...SOME THINGS!

I must Not Switch off the Gravity for Fun
I must Not Switch off the Gravity for Fun
I must Not Switch off the Gravity for Fun
I must Not Switch off th...

THAT'S ENOUGH, CLASS...! YOU MAY GO NOW...

AT LAST!

WHAP!

SWISH!

AREN'T THE DOORS SUPPOSED TO OPEN BEFORE I RUN INTO THEM?

GIVE 'EM A CHANCE, SPOTTY!

WHAP!

IN THE SHIP'S CANTEEN...

DINNER, COMPUTER, READY...

I WANT BANGERS AND MASH WITH BAKED BEANS!

SPLUTCH!

...ON A PLATE!

SHEESH! THE FOOD DOESN'T GET ANY BETTER, DOES IT?

I KNOW! I ASKED FOR PIZZA!

AND IT'S NOT JUST THE FOOD THAT'S BORING! LOOK AT ALL THIS OUTER SPACE!

IT JUST GOES ON AND ON AND ON AND ON...

...WHEN IS SOMETHING GOING TO HAPPEN?!

KLUNK

WHAT WAS THAT?!

DUNNO!

MAYBE WE HIT AN ASTEROID!

AND, THEN AGAIN, MAYBE NOT...

THERE IS A MESSAGE FROM BASHSTREET COMMAND..!

SIGH..! PUT IT ON SCREEN!

AAH...TEACHER! HOW LOVELY TO SEE YOU!

UH-OH...

I'LL COME STRAIGHT TO THE POINT..!

WE HAVE A DANGEROUS PROBLEM...

...AND WE WANT YOUR CADETS TO FIX IT!

BUT, SIR... THEY'RE ONLY KIDS!

OH, COME ON! THEY MUST BE ABLE TO DO SOMETHING!

BURP!

YAAY!

THAT MUST BE THE WINNER!

CLAP! CLAP! CL

WAIT! I HAVEN'T DONE MINE YET!

OKAY ... LOTS OF AIR...

SUCK!

SUCK!

SWISH!

BURP!

TOOTS? WHAT ON...

JUST PRACTISING MY ALIEN LANGUAGES, SIR!

OH, VERY WELL ...

CADETS, TO THE BRIEFING ROOM ...

WE HAVE A MISSION...!

IN THE BRIEFING ROOM...

NOW ... ARE WE ALL READY?

WHY IS IT SO DARK?

COMPUTER! ACTIVATE HOLOGRAM!

ZZZZMMMMMM

WOW!

COOL!

WHAT IS THAT?

AN ALIEN FROM THE PLANET RUMPUS 4..!

IT LOOKS LIKE PLUG ON A BAD DAY!

NOW THESE ALIENS HAVE KIDNAPPED ONE OF OUR SCIENTISTS...

PAF!

OUR MISSION IS TO RESCUE HIM!

'ERBERT, TAKE THE SHIP INTO ORBIT AROUND THE PLANET..!

WHAT PLANET?

?!

DANNY, TAKE OVER FROM 'ERBERT... ...QUICK!

YOU GOT IT!

WE'RE IN ORBIT, SIR!

GREAT! TOOTS, OPEN COMMU- NICATIONS!

AYE, AYE, TEACH!

THIS IS TEACHER OF THE STARSHIP 'BASH-STREET'!...

WE BRING GREETINGS FROM EARTH...!

THIS IS ZARG OF RUMPUS 4...

GO AWAY OR WE'LL SHOOT!

THEY'RE NOT VERY FRIENDLY, ARE THEY?

GRRRRRRRRRRRRR...

BEAM US UP, TEACH!

...HUH?!

I COULD HAVE THOUGHT OF THAT!

BUT YOU DIDN'T, DID YOU...!

HHMMMMMMMMMMMMMMMM...

MEANWHILE...

ZAAAAP!

HEH! HEH! THE LASER STILL WORKS ON THE BUILDINGS!

YEAH...! YOU'RE NOT AS STUPID AS YOU LOOK!

WHAT'S THAT SUPPOSED TO MEAN?!

RUMBLE! RUMBLE!

RASH!

I HAVE A REALLY GOOD ANSWER TO THAT ONE!

THERE THEY ARE!

NOW WHAT?!

I'LL BLAST A HOLE IN THIS WALL!

ZZZZZ PHFUT!

AND SO...

TEACHER'S LOG, STARDATE ...

WOULD YOU STOP THAT ?!

SIDNEY'S STILL DOWN ON THE PLANET !

YEAH...! BEAM HIM BACK UP !

THAT WON'T BE POSSIBLE, I'M AFRAID...

WE HAVE NOW BLOCKED YOUR BEAMING SIGNAL...!

YOUR FRIEND IS STAYING RIGHT HERE !

YOU FIEND !

LOOK..! HE'S STILL GOT HIS LITTLE GUN !

HA! HA! HA! HA! HA! HA! HA

WHY DON'T YOU SHOOT ME, HMMM ?

TEACHER'S LOG, STARDATE: MONDAY EVENING...

ZARG AND THE ALIENS HAVE PROMISED NOT TO BE SO NAUGHTY IN FUTURE...

THEY'RE EVEN WRITING A PEACE TREATY!

AFTER A BUSY DAY, WE ARE LEAVING RUMPUS 4...

WELL... SORT OF...

"RESISTANCE IS USELESS", YOU SAID! "WE CAN CONQUER THE UNIVERSE", YOU SAID...!

SHUT UP AND WRITE!

We Musst Not Kidnapp Sientists from EARth
We Musst Not Kidnapp Sientists from EARth
We Musst Not Kidnapp Sientists from EARth
We Musst Not Kidnapp Sientists from EARth
We Musst Not Kidnapp Sientists from EARth
We Musst Not Kidnapp Sientists from EARth
We Musst Not Kidnapp Sientists from EARE!

MEANWHILE, I'VE LET SOMEONE ELSE TAKE COMMAND...

HOW'S IT GOING, CAPTAIN?

EVERYTHING'S UNDER CONTROL!

YOUR DRINK, SIR!

YOUR BEANO, SIR!

READY TO LEAVE ORBIT, CAPTAIN BIGHEAD!

The BASH STREET KIDS in "A FUNNY OLD GAME"

Hi, there! Super-Smooth Les Dynam here, welcoming you to a brand new football season.

This programme will bring you thrills and excitement every week...

...and that's just having the good fortune to admire ME on your screens, you lucky people...!

The season kicks off with today's 'Hilarity Shield' match between two evenly matched sides...

Yeah! They're both rubbish.

...So it's over to our match commentator, John Wotson at Trembly Stadium...

Thank you, Des! Here at Trembly Stadium the atmosphere's absolutely buzzing!

BZZZ BZZZZ BZZZ BZZZZ BZZZ BZZZZ

Dat's not atmosphere! Dat's my best bees wot is buzzin'!

BZZZZZZZ ZZZZZZZZ

So now, let us welcome our first team...

...THE BEANO ALL-STARS.

HURRAY!

...and their opponents, The Bash Street Kids.

Hurray...!

Today's referee will be 'Teacher' from Bash Street.

Don't you think he might be biased?

I certainly hope so!

And now for the tossing of the coin to see which team kicks off...

Oh, dear...

Goal-kick for the Beano All-stars...

WHUMP!

...Dino wins the header...

BONK!

...Plug to Danny...

...but Danny is tackled by Ball Boy!

Ball Boy's super skills get him past the Bash Street defence...!

CRASH!

AND HE SHOOTS FOR GOAL!

POW!

BLOING!

...And a beautiful... er... combined save and goal-kick from Fatty's stomach...

Cor! Look at it go!

...Dino wins the header...

BONK!

...And it's between Cuthbert and Walter! It's anybody's ball!

After you, my dear chap!

OOOH! CAN I?!

...The Beano All-Stars have possession of the ball, the score is nil-nil...

...Minnie to Ernest...

Oh, wow! Now to impress Daisy with some of my super footballing skills!

Look at this! ...and this! ...and this!

BOMP!
TAP!
BING!

Hey, Daisy! Coo-ee!

Friend of yours?

Never saw him before in my life!

CLOSED

Daisy would never refuse to go out with a great football star like me!

BIMP!
BOMP!
BAMP!

KRUMP!

Oh dear... looks like the Beano All-Stars are down to nine players...

RUMBLE!
RUMBLE! RUMBLE!
RUMBLE! RUMBLE!
RUMBLE!
RUMBLE!

Hey! where's the ball?

I thought you had it!

SCREECH!
SCREECH!

KRUMP!!

Hey, Danny! The ball's heading in that direction.

Ball Boy is beginning to annoy me!

LET'S GET HIM!!!

uh-oh!

SOMEBODY... HELP!

RUMBLE! RUMBLE!

Billy whizz to the rescue!

Danny has the ball...

...and he gets past Roger the Dodger.

Not to worry...

...I have a great dodge coming up.

...with my very own referee's whistle!

PHWEEP!

Eh? what was that for?

PHWEEP!

Eh? what was that for?

I don't KNOW, I tell you!!!

...he passes to wilfrid...

...but wilfrid is challenged by one of the Beano All-Stars!

I am...?!

SPLOTCH!

The Beano All-Stars are down to eight players... Bash Street are down to nine players, the score is still nil-nil...

Danny takes the free-kick...

BLAM!

It's 'erbert's ball!

...He gets it past the opposition's midfield...!

...he gets it past their defence...!

What a player! What a performer!

Where's HE going?

Sigh!

Well... er... we'd better use the spare ball.

What a hero! What a star!

Goal-kick for the Beano All-Stars...

WHUMP!

It's Plug's ball!

Not if I can help it!

Uh-oh! Billy Whizz!

Smiffy! Come here, QUICK!

With my Super-whizz speed...

...I'm sure to score! Chuckle!

KLOINK!

Did someone tickle my head?

Smiffy, you're so thick, you're beautiful!

Good game of football, this!

Yeah... mind you, the rules have changed a bit since my day.

TWINKLE TWINKLE, LITTLE STAR...!

Free-kick to the Beano-All Stars!

Okay, I want everyone in the Bash Street penalty area when I take this free-kick.

Ooh! I can feel a dodge coming on...

The soot from this piece of coal makes for a convincing black eye...

...now I just wait for the referee to blow the whistle and...

PHWEEP!

Aargh! I've been fouled in the penalty area!

Cuthbert's committed a foul!

Cor! There's hope for him yet!

Bash Street's new keeper takes the goal-kick...

BOOT!

Toots to Danny...

...Danny to Spotty...

...and Spotty takes the shot!

BLAM!

...and a BEAUTIFUL save by Dean of the Beano All-Stars!

PAF!

Corner to Bash Street!

CLAP! CLAP! CLAP! CLAP!

Okay? Plug... you know what to do?!

Aye, aye, captain!

James, get to the near post. Try not to let the ball get past you.

Excuse me...

TAP! TAP!

What is it?

BLEAUUGH!

Shriek! I want my mummy!

Goal!

Bash Street have Scored!

... and the crowd is going wild?

Are you going to allow that goal?

Of course! There's nothing in the rules about pulling faces!

We've got to think of something, Dennis! We're running out of time!

Not to mention players...

GIBBER! GIBBER!

Okay! I'll take over from Dean as goalie...

...but how do we protect ourselves from Plug's ugly face?

I know! Let's play with our jerseys pulled over our heads!

It was only a suggestion...

Dennis! I've just has a minxwave!

Whisper... whisper... whisper... whisper...

Why, Min... that's positively wicked!

And so...

BLAM!

POW!

Corner to Bash Street!

Plug...?

Your wish is my command!

James, get to the near post. Try not to let the ball get past you.

Excuse me...

What is it...?

BLEAAH!

AAAiiiiEEE

CRASH!

PING!

Isn't it amazing what Dennis can stuff up his jumper?

Yes... doing his laundry is an adventure!

Well, that's Plug out of the game!

Yeah... I remember once when I saw him pulling faces...

GIBBER! GIBBER!

...It took me days to recover...

Where's Ball Boy off to in such a hurry?

Ball Boy's making a run...

...he's found space...

BOOT!

Nice ball, Dennis!

AAAARGH!

Ball Boy has a clear run for goal...

Come on... come on...!

...But the Bash Street Kids are catching him up!

Over here, Ball Boy!

Good man, James!

Go on, James! Take it all the way!!!

RUMBLE! RUMBLE!

KRUMP!

well... here we go again...!

RUMBLE! RUMBLE! RUMBLE..!

...But Bash Street are too late.

This is my moment of glory!

My luck has changed at last!

KLONK!

Sheesh!

He's not called Calamity James for nothing is he?

Free-kick to the Beano All-Stars.

How come?

We never touched James!

And I suppose Ball Boy ran himself over, eh?

Trust you to be so picky!

which means that the only player left on the pitch...

...is Winston from Bash Street.

Winston has a clear run for goal.

...But time is running out!

...Come on... come on...

Come on... come on...

INHALE!

ICE

PUNT!

PHWEEP!

GOAL!

So the final score is – Bash Street – 2... Beano All-Stars – 1!

I think I've gone allergic to cats!

Me too...

Can I have everyone's attention, please?!

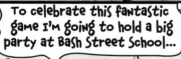

To celebrate this fantastic game I'm going to hold a big party at Bash Street School...

...and everyone's invited!!!

HURRAY!

AND SO...

ALL RIGHT, CLASS... GEOGRAPHY TEXT BOOKS OUT, PLEASE.

BOO!

HISS!

BORING..!

WHY CAN'T YOU TEACH SOMETHING USEFUL?

SUCH AS?

LIKE HOW TO FIND A WINNING CONKER.!

OR HOW TO MAKE TOFFEE LAST FOREVER!

OR HOW TO GET YOUR FOOT OVER YOUR HEAD.

NO! I'VE GOT A GOOD ONE!

PARP!

...TEACH US HOW TO BE HAPPY..!

YEAH..!

BRILLIANT..!

BUT... I CAN'T TEACH YOU HOW TO BE HAPPY.

WHY NOT?

BECAUSE I DON'T KNOW MYSELF.

YOU HAVE TO KNOW SOMETHING BEFORE YOU CAN TEACH IT?

NEWS TO ME...!

WELL, THEN! WE'LL TEACH YOU!

COME ON...!

TRAMPLE!

TRAMPLE!

TRAMPLE!

TRAMPLE!

TRAMPLE

TRA

SIGH..!

3

ON THE PLAYING FIELDS...

OKAY, LESSON NUMBER ONE IN BEING HAPPY: HAVE FUN!

HAVE... FUN?

YEAH! DO FUN THINGS!

COME ON, EVERYONE! LET'S SHOW HIM!

LOOK! I CAN STAND ON MY HEAD!

AND I CAN JUMP BACKWARDS!

AND I'M GONNA RIDE A COW!

?

MOO!

WELL, GEE UP THEN!

OKAY, TEACH... YOUR TURN!

RIGHT... ..HAVE FUN...

CRASH!

HOP!

PATHETIC.

THIS IS GOING TO BE HARDER THAN I THOUGHT.

?

COME ON, TEACH!

LOOSEN UP!

BIFF! WALLOP! BANG!

GEE UP, YOU SILLY MOO!

④

AND SO...

HERE WE ARE!

WHERE BETTER FOR FUN THAN A PLAYGROUND?

LET'S START WITH SOMETHING SIMPLE.

ER... SPOTTY...

OKAY, READY?

CREAK! CREAK!

SHOVE!

RIDE 'EM, COWBOY!

WHAP! WHAP! WHAP! WHAP! WHAP! WHAP! WHAP!

PERHAPS NOT, EH?

WHERE AM I...?

WHAT'S NEXT, DANNY?

ER... OVER HERE!

AND SO...

BOO HOO HOO...!

COME ON, TEACH! THIS ONE'S EASY!

YEAH! ALL YOU'VE GOT TO DO IS SLIDE DOWN!

CREAK! CREAK!

CREE-E-EAK!

PYOING!

CRASH!

I WANT MY MUMMY...!

ANOTHER FAILURE...

I THOUGHT GROWN-UPS WERE SUPPOSED TO BE CLEVER?!

⑥

THE END

10

FIRST UP WAS IVY THE TERRIBLE...

I'M GONNA SING A 'BEATLES' SONG!

ALL RIGHT, YOU MAY BEGIN...

ER... WHAT DO WE HAVE TO DO..?

JUST LISTEN TO HER SING AND THEN SAY WHAT YOU THINK OF IT...

POP IDIOTS

SHE LOVES YOU! YEAH! YEAH! YEAH..!

DO WE LOVE HER?

NO...

NO...

NO..!

POP IDIOTS

THEN BALL BOY...

WE ARE GONNA WIN THE CUP..!

OH NO, YOU'RE NOT!

NEXT!

POP IDIOTS

WALTER THE SOFTY...

RAINDROPS ON SNOWDROPS AND...

STOP!

THAT'S THE MOST AWFUL THING I'VE EVER HEARD!

BOO HOO HOO..!

YOU MADE HIM CRY!

YEAH..! I'M REALLY GETTING THE HANG OF THIS!

POP IDIOTS

②

NEXT UP: MINNIE THE MINX...!

OH, I'M MINXING THE NIGHT AWAY...!

CLICK! CLICK! TAP! TAP!

BOO..! GET OFF!

SPLAT!

ER... HEADMASTER, YOU MIGHT BE TAKING THIS A LITTLE TOO FAR...

BUT SHE WAS RUBBISH!

SPLAT!

!

SO... DOES ANYONE ELSE THINK I WAS RUBBISH..?

TWANG! TWANG!

ER... NO!

I LIKED IT!

YOU'RE THROUGH...!

POP IDIOTS

HEH! HEH!

THAT WAS CHEATING!

YEAH...!

I WISH I'D THOUGHT OF IT...

NEXT: CALAMITY JAMES...

TRIP!

OOF!

OOPS..! SORRY ABOUT...

13

CLONK!

13

ER... WAS THAT IT?

WELL, I'VE SEEN ENOUGH...

NEXT!

0   0

IDIOTS

③

NEXT UP WAS ROGER THE DODGER...

HERE'S A LITTLE SONG BY ELVIS PRESLEY...

WHO?

HE WAS A SINGER, HEADMASTER...

ARE YOU LONESOME TONIGHT...? DO YOU MISS ME TONIGHT...?

WOW...! HE'S GOOD!

VERY GOOD...!

HMM...

POP

SNIFF!

...HE'S A LITTLE TOO GOOD...

TELL ME DEAR...

TUG!

...ARE YOU LONESOME TONIGHT...?

AHEM...!

SO...! IT WAS A DODGE ALL ALONG!

CAN I THROW A TOMATO AT HIM?

NEXT, BILLY WHIZZ...

WITH A SONG AT WHIZZ-SPEED...!

ALL RIGHT... YOU MAY BEGIN...!

I JUST FINISHED!

ZZZZZ

I CAN DO IT AGAIN IF YOU...

NEXT!

LES PRETEND...

HERE'S A LITTLE SONG BY ELVIS PRE...

NEXT!

POP

SHEESH...! I DIDN'T THINK THEY WOULD BE THAT TOUGH!

SPLAT!

⑤

SO ... THOSE WERE THE QUALIFYING ROUNDS ...

...AND NOW "DENNIS AND THE DIN-MAKERS" AND "THE BASH STREET KIDS" WILL COMPETE FOR ...

HEY...! HAVEN'T YOU FORGOTTEN SOMEBODY?!

WHO?

WELL, WHAT ABOUT ..??

...MEEEEEEEEeeeee...

NOW THAT'S A GOOD IDEA ...

I WISH WE'D THOUGHT OF IT...

AS I WAS SAYING... WE WILL COMPETE AND YOU WILL VOTE FOR THE BEST!

HOW'S YOUR BIT OF FLOOR?

SO, FIRST, HERE ARE ... THE BASH STREET KIDS!

OH..!

ALL RIGHT...! SHIRTS OFF!

BADUMP!

OH NO...

NOT AGAIN ...

GET READY TO PULL THE TRAP-DOORS ON MY SIGNAL...

OKAY..!

HYUK! HYUK!

7

⑨

OH! HELLO, TEACHER!... I DIDN'T SEE YOU THERE!

EVIDENTLY.

HEY, TEACH! HAVE YOU SEEN THE 'HARRY POTTER' FILM?

NO, BUT I HAVE READ THE BOOK.

THERE'S A BOOK?

ALL RIGHT, CLASS! ENGLISH TEXT BOOKS OUT, PLEASE!

ENGLISH FOR BORING OLD F...

TODAY'S LESSON WILL BE ON ENGLISH GRAMMAR.

OH, WHOOPEE...

CAN'T WE LEARN SOME MAGIC?

YEAH! LIKE HARRY POTTER!

DON'T BE SILLY!

NOW PAY ATTENTION, CLASS...

... WE WILL BEGIN ON PAGE THIRTY-ONE WITH THE SECTION ON VERBS...

I WISH WE COULD HAVE HAD A LESSON ON MAGIC!

ME TOO!

...MOST ENGLISH VERBS HAVE PRE-DICTABLE FORMS, APART FROM THE IRREGULAR VERBS...

...TO FORM PAST TENSE AND PAST PARTICIPLE. NEARLY ALL COMBINE THE INFINITIVE WITH THE LETTERS '-ED' AS IN 'LOOKED'. BUT THERE ARE MORE THAN A HUNDRED VERBS, INCLUDING SOME OF THE COMMONEST, WITH UNPREDICTABLE FORMS OF PAST TENSE AND PARTICIPLE...

OPINIONS DIFFER AS TO WHERE TO PUT IN INVERTED COMMAS AND FULL STOPS AT THE END OF SENTENCES. BUT AN ALTERNATIVE ARRANGEMENT IS TO PUT THE FULL STOPS OUTSIDE OF QUOTATION MARKS SO THAT THE READER IS CLEAR THAT... TRYING TO COMMUNICATE WITH SUFFICIENT CLARITY, BEARING IN MIND THAT THE RULES OF CORRECT GRAMMAR ARE THERE TO HELP THE READER, NOT ACT AS A KIND OF BARRIER...

BONK!

THERE IS AN OLD DISPUTE ABOUT SPLIT INFINITIVES WHICH SHOULD HAVE BEEN SETTLED LONG AGO. THE ISSUE IS WHETHER AN FULL INFINITIVE SUCH AS 'TO BE' SHOULD BE SPLIT BY AN ADVERB SUCH AS 'TO SUDDENLY BE'...

ZZZZZ...!

MMMM...!

SNORE...!

ZZZZ...!

GLBLBLBL...!

THE HYPHEN, CONSISTING OF HALF A DASH, INDICATES AND AIDS CLARITY BY LINKING ADJACENT WORDS TO EACH OTHER. ENGLISH DIFFERS FROM A RELUCTANCE TO USE SUCH GRAMMATICAL TERMS WITHIN THE BOUNDS OF GOOD WRITING...

THE EXCLAMATION MARK IS NO...

T'WOO?

THE SIMPLEST STYLE... TO USE... IS PERFECTLY EVEN...

T'WIT- T'WOOO...!

②

PING!

POC!

WOW! THIS IS WELL COOL!

HEY! LOOK AT ME!

ER... ...SPOTTY...

RAAHCK!

OH, HEAVENS!

TIME TO GO...!

RAAHCK!

AT THE SCHOOL...

I SAY!...WHO IS MAKING ALL THIS NOISE?!

URK!

OH... HELLO, HEADMASTER!

HOW DARE YOU FLY INTO MY OFFICE WITHOUT KNOCKING!

SORRY...

WELL, 'SORRY' ISN'T GOOD ENOUGH! YOU'RE IN SERIOUS TROUBLE, YOUNG...

AAARGH! CRASH! THUMP! BANG!

PAF! WHACK! RAAHCK! KWING!

AAH...PERHAPS BROOMSTICK FLYING IS A LITTLE BIT ADVANCED FOR YOU AT THIS STAGE....!

4

AND SO, TEACHER ORGANISED A LESSON ON MAGIC POTIONS...

NOW, I WANT YOU ALL TO WORK IN PAIRS...

EYES OF NEWTS

FILLET OF FENNY SNAKE

MAYONAISE

...AND BE SURE TO FOLLOW YOUR POTION RECIPES CAREFULLY.

COR! SOME OF THESE INGREDIENTS ARE *GROSS*!

YEAH..!

MMMM...! WHAT'S THIS, PLUG?

IT'S A 'POTION OF TRANSFORMATION'.

SO IF PLUG DRINKS IT, HE BECOMES GOOD-LOOKING!

HUH! I DON'T NEED MAGIC TO MAKE *ME* GOOD-LOOKING!

NO, YOU NEED A MIRACLE!

I'LL MAKE YOU REGRET THAT, YOU SPECKLED DWARF!

HEY, FATTY! GIVE ME THE ...

AAAH!

...FATTY'S A PIG..!

SO TELL US SOMETHING WE DON'T KNOW!

ALL RIGHT, ALL RIGHT! TEACHER TO THE RESCUE!

OH, BE CAREFUL OF OUR...

CRASH!

...POTION OF INVISIBILITY!

5

WELL, REALLY!

I DO HATE IT WHEN THEY SERVE THE 'AFTERS' BEFORE WE'VE FINISHED THE MAIN COURSE!

ME TOO!

LISTEN, YOU LOT!...DON'T LOOK UP WHATEVER YOU DO!

PIE

WHY NOT?

SLAP!

AAAAH!!

THEY'RE NOT VERY POLITE, ARE THEY?

NO...

...WHY DON'T WE TEACH THEM SOME MANNERS...?

YE-E-EAH...!

OO-ER...!

I DIDN'T LIKE THE SOUND OF THAT!

OINK!

AND *YOU* CAN SHUT UP AN' ALL!

READY...?

YES!

...THEN LET THEM HAVE IT !!!

AHEM!...MOST ENGLISH VERBS HAVE PREDICTABLE FORMS, APART FROM THE...

...TO CREATE PAST TENSE AND PAST PARTICIPLE...

FULL STOPS SHOULD BE USED ONLY WHEN A SENTENCE IS...

ENGLISH
FOR
BORING

HEY! IT'S OUR ENGLISH LESSON!

IN TRIPLICATE!

HOLY BALONY! THAT DRAGON IS GOING TO BORE US TO DEATH!

STOP! STOP! STOP!

?

8